A Mat

by Michael Powell
illustrated by Jamie Smith

Practice Decodable 8

McGraw Hill Education

Bothell, WA • Chicago, IL • Columbus, OH • New York, NY

MHEonline.com

Send all inquiries to:
McGraw-Hill Education
8787 Orion Place
Columbus, OH 43240

ISBN: 978-0-02-145987-2
MHID: 0-02-145987-8

Printed in the United States of America.

6 7 8 CTM 23

I have a mat.

Sam sat on a mat.

Tam sat.

Matt sat.

Can I?

I sat on a mat!